Animal Smarts

SYLVIA FUNSTON

Owl

Owl Books are published by Greey de Pencier Books Inc.,
370 King St. West, Suite 300, Toronto, Ontario M5V 1J9

The Owl colophon is a trademark of Owl Children's Trust Inc.
Greey de Pencier Books Inc. is a licensed user of trademarks of Owl Children's Trust Inc.

Distributed in the United States by Firefly Books (U.S.) Inc.,
230 Fifth Avenue, Suite 1607, New York, NY 10001.

This book was published with the generous support
of the Canada Council and the Ontario Arts Council.

Dedication
To Ena, for all her loving help

Cataloguing in Publication Data

Funston, Sylvia
        Animal smarts

(The secret life of animals)
Includes index.
ISBN 1-895688-66-3 (bound)   ISBN 1-895688-67-1 (pbk.)

1. Animal intelligence – Juvenile literature. I. Title.
II. Series.

QL785.F86 1997   j591.51   C96-932528-2

Design & Art Direction: Julia Naimska
Illustrations by Pat Stevens

Photo credits
Front cover, Renee Lynn/Davis Lynn; pages 4, 11, 23, Dick Haneda; 5, back cover, Sylvia Funston; 6–7, Bill Ivy;
8–9 (bottom), Art Wolfe/Tony Stone; 9, 13, Fred Bavendam/Valan; 10, Peter Weimann/Animals Animals; 14, A.
Shoob/University of Tel Aviv; 14–15, Dr. Christopher Boesch/University of Basel; 16–17, J.D. Taylor/Bill Ivy; 18,
J.A. Wilkinson/Valan; 19, Stephen J. Krasemann/DRK; 20, Wayne Lankinen/DRK; 21, Hans Reinhard/Bruce
Coleman; 22, Steve Maslowski/Valan; 25, Frans Lanting/Minden; 26, Don & Pat Valenti/DRK; 27, Dr. Graham
Stone/Oxford University; 28–29, Chris Johns/National Geographic; 30, Heather Angel; 31, Jeff Foott/Valan;
32–33, Jim Balog/Jupiter; 34–35, Gerard Lacz/Animals Animals; 37, Alan Levenson; 38–39, Michael
Nichols/Magnum; 40 (bottom), Dick Hemingway; 40–41, Mark Moffett/Minden; 41 (bottom), Max Gibbs/Oxford
Scientific Films; 42, Gerard Lacz/NHPA; 43, London Scientific Films/Oxford Scientific Films; 44, 44–45, Michael
Goldman; 46, 47, Sally Boysen/Ohio State University.

Printed in Hong Kong

C   D   E   F

Contents

Secret Smarts

My family used to live in an apartment building where visitors called us from a phone in the lobby to let us know they had arrived. If the phone in our apartment rang once it was a telephone call, but if it rang twice it meant that someone was calling to be let in. Our bulldog, Jigs (shown below), took only about three days to figure the whole thing out, and he would leap for joy whenever he heard the double ring.

How did Jigs know that one ring meant he could go on snoozing, but two rings meant someone would walk through the front door? Can Jigs count up to two? Or is he just a good observer? Maybe we gave him clues by acting a certain way when we heard two rings.

Do animals think? To find out, researchers study how animals behave. For instance, a researcher at the Metropolitan Toronto Zoo set up an experiment to test how well a gorilla named Charles (opposite page) could remember where to find food. Every day, she hid eight containers in Charles's enclosure, but only four of them contained any food. Charles quickly caught on to the routine. After he found food in four containers, he wouldn't even bother opening the rest of the containers! Charles could count up to four. But nobody taught him how to do it.

So maybe Jigs can count to two. To make sure, we could try Charles's experiment on him. But how can we train Jigs to open containers without chewing them up? Solving that problem might tell us about human smarts as well as animal smarts.

Once upon a time, in a laboratory far away, a raven proved he could count up to six. "So what?" you might say. Try counting without using any words for the numbers and see how far you get. As the largest member of the very smart crow family, ravens are no bird brains. They have three things in common with most animals that we know have active minds. They lead a hectic social life, they always keep an eye open for new things to eat, and they're curious about absolutely everything.

WHO'S SMART?

Group Think

How many things in your life make you think, or teach you things, or give your brain a workout? There are probably so many you can hardly count them. In the same way, there are a lot of things that affect how smart an animal is. One clue to animal smarts seems to be group living.

It takes practice to learn rules of group living, and it takes brain power to remember who is part of your group and who isn't. There's a lot to keep track of when you live in a group — who's who in the group, how you should act with others, and if someone owes you a favor (like extra food). And the bigger the group, the harder your brain has to work. Some of the smartest animals — chimpanzees, dolphins, crows, even honeybees — have to get along with each other, just as humans do.

Wolves live in packs with male and female leaders, known as the alpha pair. How an alpha wolf treats the rest of the pack while it's in charge determines how they'll treat it when it's no longer leader of the pack. If the alpha wolf treated the pack kindly, it will be treated well. But if it abused the pack, it had better watch out. Wolves have keen memories when it comes to who did what to whom.

When male elephants are fully grown, they leave the herd they grew up in. But a female elephant stays with her mother, sisters and female cousins in the same herd for her whole life. Eventually, she learns all the rules and customs of the group. She gets experience as a babysitter, and learns to help other members of her herd. She knows, for example, that if one of the herd is injured, everyone has to slow down so the hurt elephant can keep up. If a female elephant learns enough, one day she might even be the wise, old granny that leads the herd.

Since group living is only one of the things that might help develop an animal's brain, there are exceptions. The giant octopus is a loner that's smart. In one case, an octopus outsmarted two scientists. They had built a see-through maze with doors. At one end of the maze they placed an octopus treat, at the other end the octopus. The octopus was supposed to learn which doors opened inwards and which opened outwards so it could reach the food. But the octopus found a better way. It looked at the maze, paused, then lifted the maze out of the way and rushed underneath it to grab the food! The scientists weighted down the maze and tried again. Left with no choice, the octopus figured out which doors to pull and which ones to push to get at the food.

Brain Food

If living in groups makes you smart, how do you explain howler monkeys and spider monkeys? Spider monkeys spend their days alone and only get together at night, but they are smarter than the howlers who spend their whole day in a group. Could it be a case of "You are what you eat?"

Howlers greet the dawn with a chorus of ear-splitting howls. Then they go off together in search of food, over an area of forest the size of about ten city blocks. The group seems to have a good sense of direction and a shared memory of which plants have the best leaves. For howler monkeys, food is nothing but leaves.

Spider monkeys recognize a lot more than leaves as food. A group of them would strip a tree bare of fruit in no time, so they split up each morning and get back together again at night. Each spider monkey has to remember about 100 kinds of fruit and where to find them on thousands of trees spread over ten times the area covered by howlers.

Having to memorize all those things gives a spider monkey's brain a lot of exercise. When you combine it with grouping together at night, eating fruit seems to make a spider monkey smarter than eating leaves does for a howler monkey. Maybe you could say that a spider monkey's diet has gone straight to its head.

For the "vampire" finch of the Galapagos Islands, it's a case of "You are what you drink." Fresh water is in such short supply that this little bird finds a much bigger bird and pecks at it until there's enough blood to sip. The larger bird probably thinks the finch is removing hard-to-budge ticks, because it doesn't seem to mind what's going on. Just how the finch discovered that this warm, salty liquid makes a good, though unusual, substitute for water remains a mystery.

For months, a scientist ate his lunch in front of howler monkeys (right), who showed no interest, even when he smacked his lips and made *yum yum* sounds. But he had a hard time defending his peanut butter and banana sandwiches from spider monkeys (opposite page), who recognize a treat when they see one.

Spider monkeys aren't the only brainy creatures that eat fruit. Most gorillas eat fruit for a main course and then have insects, buds, flowers, fungus and bark for dessert. They avoid the tough-to-digest leaves that grow in tropical forests. But the gorillas that live near the Virunga Volcanoes in Rwanda and Zaire do eat leaves because fruit is scarce. Are these gorillas any less intelligent than their fruit-eating cousins? Apparently not. The plants they eat give them the kind of challenge that give brain cells lots of exercise. How would you eat "sticky Willie" — a long-stemmed plant that's covered in hundreds of hooks — without getting it stuck all over you? A Virunga gorilla solves this sticky problem by first rolling up the plant's long stems into a solid ball against its chin. Then it uses its teeth like a chopping knife to slice through the ball.

Wolves are smart hunters with different strategies for hunting mountain sheep on rocky slopes, caribou on flat tundra or mice in grassy meadows. Wolves eat mostly meat, but are always open to other food. They herd fish into pools, or snap them from the bank with their sharp teeth. They might even eat leftovers from other predators' meals, or chomp a mouthful of insects.

WHAT IS INSTINCT?

Just like you knew how to crawl and then walk, a whooping crane performs a complicated mating dance without ever being taught how. It's as if it sees the dance steps in its mind and all it has to do is copy them. Scientists call this kind of behavior instinctive. It springs from inner knowledge the bird was born with, and isn't something it has to learn by trial and error.

Complicated actions that get a task done — attracting a mate, building a nest or raising young — are usually instinctive. Why? If animals are born knowing how to do necessary things, they don't have to spend time and energy learning how. That leaves only behaviors that don't mean life or death to be learned.

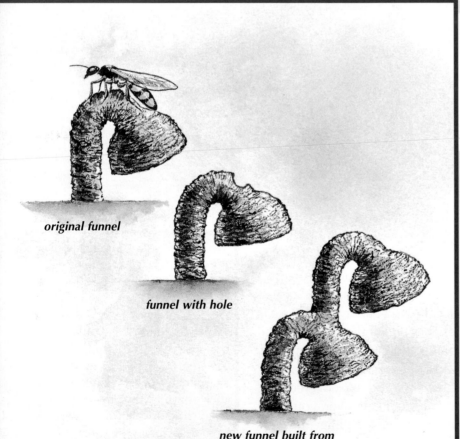

original funnel

funnel with hole

new funnel built from hole in original funnel

The Australian digger wasp lays its eggs in a tunnel and builds a mud funnel at the opening to keep out predators. Scientists poked a hole in a wasp's funnel to see if building the funnel was instinctive. If the wasp was actually thinking about what it was doing, it would patch the hole. But the wasp couldn't get beyond its instinct. A hole could be only one thing — the opening to its nest, which must be protected by a funnel. So the wasp built a second funnel around the hole in the first funnel. And it probably would build funnel upon funnel as long as the scientists kept poking holes.

If you rolled a goose egg out of its nest, the goose would roll it back in. But if you placed a grapefruit near the same goose, she'd roll that into her nest too. She's just reacting instinctively to a round object. Her "I can't help myself" behavior saves her the trouble of trying to figure out if anything shaped like an egg close to her nest is an egg or not. To make sure her young survive, it's better to sit on any egg-shaped object than to risk losing an egg.

Just because an animal acts on instinct, however, doesn't mean that it's not thinking about what it's doing. And if an animal comes across a problem that instinct can't solve, it might piece together things it already knows in a new way and come up with a brain wave.

This marine crab doesn't have sharp claws or big teeth, so it can't really fight back if it's attacked. Instead, it grabs two sea anemones and waves their stinging tentacles in its enemy's face. Did the crab figure out how to use the anemones as weapons? Or is it just acting on instinct to protect itself? Most scientists think the crab must be acting instinctively, even though it might seem that the crab realizes what it's doing and why it's doing it.

Curious Creatures

It might have killed the cat, but curiosity turned the rat into an archeologist's best friend. Rats love collecting things: buttons, scraps of wallpaper or pieces of dinner plate. These things found in ancient rats' nests have given archeologists clues to the way people lived long ago. The keen curiosity that leads rats to hoard unusual items also allows them to be smart in new and challenging situations.

This black rat (above) lives in the Jerusalem pine forests, where the only food is found deep inside tightly packed pine cones. It has survived by figuring out how to get seeds out of these pine cones by removing rows of scales in the correct order. Only black rats that live in the pine forests know how; farm and town rats don't. To find out if forest rats are born with this skill or learn it, scientists placed newborn forest rat babies with farm rats, town rats and other forest rats to raise. The forest rat babies raised by farm and town rats scored F in pine cone stripping. The forest rat babies raised by forest rat foster parents scored A+. Amazingly, forest rat mothers were doing what we used to think only primates such as humans, chimps and orangutans could do: they were teaching their young how to survive. Now, that's smart.

This baby chimpanzee is curious enough to taste the berries it has just seen its mother eating. Apart from being a safe way to learn which foods are good to eat, copying mom will also teach the young chimp which plants to eat as medicines when it's sick. Chimps have been seen swallowing the bitter leaves of the Aspilia plant, which contain a powerful antibiotic and also kill parasites. The "medicine" seems to even work against viruses in the same group as the AIDS virus.

WHO'S THINKING?

Think about it. Some animals, like dolphins, are very smart. But how much do we really know about the *way* they think? Do they think the way humans do? Trying to answer these questions, scientists look at two things: brains and behavior. They compare the way animal brains are built and carefully watch how animals solve problems they've never met before. And scientists have made some surprising discoveries. . . .

All in Your Head

Except for the blue whale, the largest animal ever, most animals alive today are tiny compared to the huge dinosaurs of prehistoric times. But while animal bodies, in general, have been shrinking, animal brains have been growing bigger. The human brain has grown faster and become more complex than any other brain. In fact, if all the animals in the world were the same size, so that you could measure brain size compared to body size, you'd see that you've got the biggest brain of any animal on Earth.

But it's not just the size of your brain that makes you smarter than, say, your dog. What gives you extra smarts is the large thinking area that includes all the wrinkles and furrows on the outside of your brain. That and the fact that your densely packed brain cells connect in more ways than the cells in any other animal's brain.

Many animal brains — such as those of dolphins, magpies and cats — are made of the same kind of cells as your brain, and are built in ways a lot like it. They have areas to handle the information coming in from the senses, and they have areas that make decisions based on the information. And why would animals have thinking areas in their brains if they didn't use them to think?

What does the magpie (opposite) have in common with the dolphin on the previous page? If you could wave a magic wand over them both and make them your size, they'd both have brains almost as big as yours! Next time you call someone a bird brain, think about the fact that a cat given the same growth spell would end up with a brain only one-third the size of yours.

If you want your kitten to become a genius cat, play with it a lot in a messy room. Playing is great exercise for the brain, so the more action your kitten's brain gets, the more connections form between its brain cells. And a study showed that the more clutter there is in a kitten's environment, the more intelligent kitty is likely to become.

Bird Brains

If you were asked what color a stick of celery and a cucumber were, you'd say they were both green, both in the same color class. Recent experiments show that most mammal and bird brains seem to work in the same way yours does when it comes to classifying things.

Pigeons were shown pictures, two at a time. Each time two new pictures appeared, one picture showed water — an ocean, a lake, a puddle, even a raindrop or a glass of water — while the other showed something that wasn't water. The pigeons learned that if they sorted what they saw into water and non-water pictures and pecked only at the water pictures, they'd receive a food reward. Soon they were pecking away at water pictures they'd never seen before, without a single mistake.

Some animals have amazingly flexible brains. Once a year, chickadees have to smarten up fast — they've hidden thousands of seeds for the winter, one by one, and now have to remember where to find them. How do they do it? They grow whole new areas of brain. Think of a chickadee's brain in computer terms — each autumn chickadees upgrade their Random Access Memory, or RAM, from 4 MB to 8 MB!

In another experiment, pigeons proved that they can use some of the same memory tricks that you do. Take "chunking." When you memorize a telephone number, you chunk it. You break a long series down into easy-to-remember pieces. Ever wonder why a telephone number looks something like this: 123 456-7890? It's because the telephone companies set them up in chunks, so they are easier to remember. Well, pigeons chunk too! At least, some did in a laboratory experiment. When they were asked to peck colors in the correct order, pigeons pecked the colors in small groups, rather than steadily in a long sequence. So it's likely that, if pigeons had telephones, the phone numbers would be in chunks, just like ours.

The brains of some songbirds like the canary (above) can actually repair themselves. When cells wear out in the song-control areas of their brains, new ones grow to take their place. Scientists study how these songbirds perform this miracle, to see if it's something that human brains might also be able to do.

Mind Maps

In a memory test, you wouldn't stand a chance against a gray squirrel. Squirrels bury nuts all over to eat later. Scientists think they use "mind maps" to retrieve hidden food. How? Imagine you're in your room; point in the direction of the fridge. You've just used a mind map to find food.

Hundreds of different types of fruit trees ripen in a tropical forest, all at different times of the year. A bird flying above the forest can easily spot which tree has ripe fruit. But orangutans live among the high branches, at the same level as the fruit hidden in the dense vegetation. How does an orangutan know when and where to find fruit that's ready for picking? It's possible that its brain contains not only a map of the forest but also a kind of fruit-picker's diary full of things like, "Today the short, twisted tree with big, glossy leaves and a broken branch will have fruit that's ripe. If I travel for three hours away from the sun at dawn I'll find it." Off it goes, slowly swinging hand over hand, straight to the tree with fruit.

To find out if gray squirrels do remember where they store nuts, instead of sniffing out buried food with their excellent sense of smell, biologists recorded the places where eight squirrels buried nuts. Then the scientists dug up the stashes and replaced the nuts. The new nuts had no tell-tale smell: they hadn't been touched by the squirrels or the scientists. Twelve days later, the squirrels went right to where they'd buried nuts and dug up the substitutes, proving they were working from memory and not from smell.

Sometimes squirrels prevent acorns from sprouting in the ground by scraping their teeth across the bottom of the acorn and killing the seed embryo inside the nut. Why bother? If an acorn sprouts before the squirrel can dig it up again, half of its food value will go to the growing seedling, instead of into the squirrel.

Behind this orangutan's high forehead is a big brain crammed with memories of how to find food in its own forest. But this super-memory will keep the orangutan supplied with food only as long as that particular forest survives. When a forest is cut down, even the world's best memory of what it contained is useless. Sadly, the deforestation of stretches of orangutan territory is one reason the orangutan is endangered.

Animal Houses

Before a house is built, an architect draws a plan called a blueprint that shows the size and shape of the house, where it will be built, the materials that will be used, and the number of doors and windows it will have. It seems some animals have similar plans in their heads for their homes.

A mental blueprint allows animals to build homes without building lessons. A beaver has a picture in its head of a lodge sitting in the middle of a deep pond. But building its home to match that picture isn't all that simple. First there has to be a pond! So the beaver piles up branches, stones and mud to form a dam that will create the pond. Has the beaver figured out that building a dam across a stream will make a pond? In any case, now it can build its lodge with a safe entrance hole deep underwater.

Prairie dogs need to keep the air fresh in their tunnels. So they build a high mound of earth around the exit hole. The air flowing across the prairie is slowed down by the mound. The fast air movement over the hole (blue arrow) and slower air movement around the hole (red arrow) make a pocket of low air pressure at the exit. This pocket sucks air all the way through the burrow from the entrance hole (purple arrow). And the mound makes a great lookout point, too.

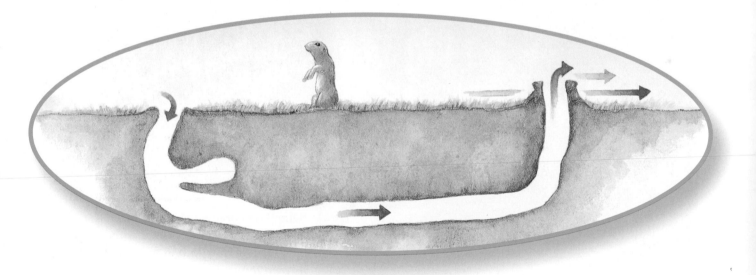

If you found yourself alone and the only building materials around were tall grasses, what kind of shelter could you build? Animals face this kind of challenge all the time. Many of them build homes that are better and stronger than anything we could make with such limited materials. And sometimes animals will see a shortcut and save time. A jackdaw's nest, for example, is big and messy, built on a strong foundation of twigs. But a female jackdaw who found an empty nesting box decided to ignore her mental blueprint of what a nest should be. Throwing away all the twigs her mate brought to her, she built a cosy nest in the box out of soft straw and newspaper.

The masked weaverbird of East Africa starts its nest by knotting several pieces of grass to hang from a branch, then knots them together at the bottom to form a strong sling. Weaving strips of grass under and over each other at a ninety degree angle, it builds a roof, walls and base around the sling. Weaverbirds have a mental blueprint for their nests, and a male weaverbird has to follow it exactly. Otherwise he won't attract a female, and he'll have to pull it apart and start again.

Buzz Brains

What about bug smarts? Most insects are so small, you're probably asking yourself how there could even be room for brains in their heads. But before you write off all insects as nonthinkers, here's the buzz. Honeybees, one of the most social insects, are probably the smartest, too.

Research shows that honeybees can plan ahead. A scientist left bee food in the form of sugar water for a hive of honeybees to find. He moved the food 25 percent farther away from the hive each day. In almost no time, the bees anticipated where the sugar water would be moved to the next day and flew straight to that spot.

To make the walls of a tree hollow waterproof, windproof and smooth enough to build a honeycomb inside, honeybees use a material called propolis, a paste they make by mixing together tree sap and resins. When honeybees in a hot region of Italy had trouble building honeycombs because their beeswax kept melting, they solved the problem in a clever way. By adding propolis to their wax, the bees raised its melting point enough to keep it solid.

Bee brains shouldn't surprise us. As you've seen, living in a group tends to make animals smarter, and many types of bees do almost everything in groups. They build hives, take care of their young, defend the nest, and find and collect food, all working together. This bee is collecting pollen from a flower and storing it on its legs to take back as food for all the bees in the hive.

Bees can even judge if information makes sense before they act on it. In one experiment, a scout bee brought news to the hive that it had found a good source of food in the middle of the lake. The hive bees responded with the bee equivalent of "Get lost!" and ignored the news. Who ever heard of bee food in the middle of a lake? But this time, they should have believed their scout instead of their own judgement. There *was* food in the lake — and it had been placed in a boat by a sneaky scientist.

Finding food is the kind of thing that a honeybee can't leave entirely to instinct. But if bees can plan and use judgement to find food, what about other tasks like mating? Among speedy little flower bees, the males wait in line to mate with a female. Scientists noticed that the bees were lined up according to size, with the biggest first in line. Was it coincidence? The scientists waved away the hovering bees. Quick as a flash, the bees lined up again in exactly the same order. There's no way to tell if this means that flower bees are actually thinking, but it does seem to show that they can classify things according to size.

Flower bees buzz around so fast that it's hard to see what they're doing. A team of scientists video-taped them so that they could run frame-by-frame replays. To identify individual bees, the scientists stuck light, numbered disks on their backs. This video still shows male bees hovering in line, waiting to mate with a female.

WHAT IS INSPIRATION?

When scientists see an animal acting "smart," they try to figure out if it's acting purely on instinct or if it's figuring things out. That's hard to do with animals in the wild. It's easier to tell in a laboratory. Then scientists can test a captive animal with a problem that it wouldn't normally meet in the wild. If it finds a solution to the problem, most scientists would agree that the animal has had a real brain wave — a flash of inspiration.

One pigeon was trained to push a box toward a green spot. It was also trained to climb on a box to peck a banana hanging directly overhead. What if you hung a banana just out of reach of that pigeon, and put a box nearby. Do you think it could put together the actions it learned separately and, in a flash of inspiration, figure out how to get at the banana? Of course, that's just what it did.

Not to be outdone by a pigeon, a chimpanzee figured out how to get at an out-of-reach banana, too. Researchers presented the chimp with the problem of food it couldn't reach, and then showed it two photographs — one of a stool and one of a hose. It chose the photo of the stool, the object that it needed to solve the problem. The pigeon worked with real objects, but the chimp had to work with the ideas of objects. Instead of pushing around a box in its cage, the chimpanzee showed that it could push ideas around in its own mind.

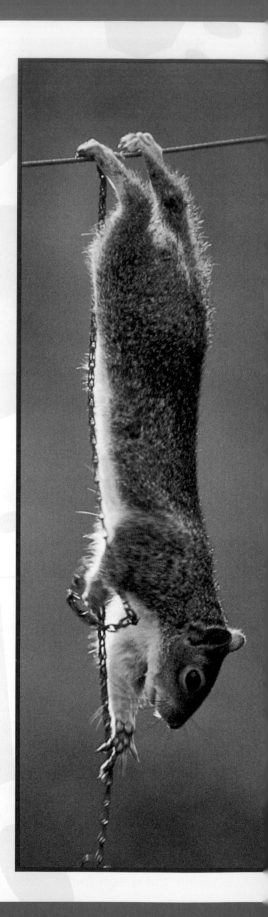

Just because a squirrel has lost its tail doesn't mean it's lost its smarts. Stumpy the gray squirrel tried for three weeks before it finally figured out how to reach a can of sunflower seeds hanging by a chain from a wire. No wonder it's almost impossible to make squirrel-proof bird feeders!

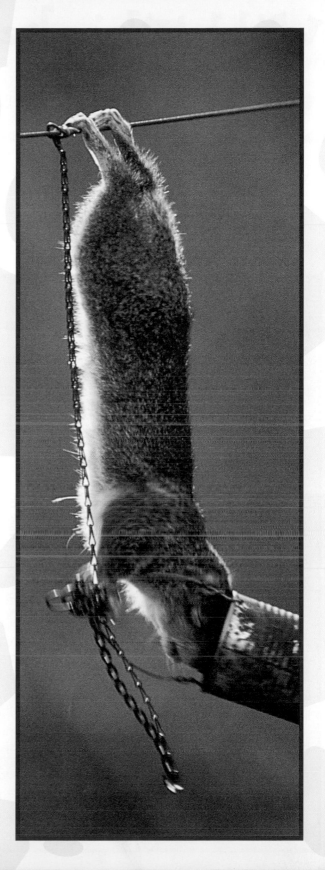

Wild Thinkers

Wild animals need smarts to survive, and often seem to show inspired thinking. But it's hard to tell from one observation of a particular animal in the wild if it is having a flash of insight or not. It could be copying another animal. Maybe it accidentally stumbled upon a solution to the problem and will never use it again. It takes careful scientific study to prove that an animal has had a brain wave to solve a problem.

Japan's snow-covered Shiga Heights mountains are a cold place for monkeys to live. So Japanese macaques often sit in mountain hot springs to keep warm. Almost 30 years ago, a female macaque named Tokiwa walked into a hotel hot pool and sat down. Now, that's a hot idea! Gradually, it caught on with other macaques. Eventually there were so many macaques warming themselves in the hotel pool that another pool had to be built so that humans would have a chance to bathe.

About forty years ago, a Japanese macaque named Imo found a new way to clean her food. First, she began washing her muddy sweet potatoes in the sea. Soon, all the macaques in Imo's group were washing their potatoes the same way. Years later Imo cleaned the sand from handfuls of wheat by tossing the wheat into the water. When the sand sank all she had to do was scoop the floating wheat off the surface.

Orangutans live, eat and move among the treetops, safely away from the ground where hunters roam. But sometimes swinging from tree to tree can be a challenge. One day a female orangutan was observed with her baby in a young, flexible tree. She wanted to cross from that tree to a larger tree that was just out of reach. She tried to swing on a branch to get close to the larger tree, but she couldn't reach. So she carefully placed her baby where its weight would bend the flexible tree they were in closer to the larger tree. This time, by swinging on a branch, she was able to grab a branch of the other tree. In a flash, she took hold of her infant and got them both safely across.

Did the orangutan and the other wild animals on these pages have a flash of inspiration? You decide.

Female killer whales teach their calves to swim right onto the beach to catch seals to eat. Two researchers saw one young whale strand itself on the shore. The mother headed out to sea, seeming to leave her calf. But then she turned and swam back at top speed, straight at her calf. At the last moment, she turned to the side, creating a huge wave that lifted the calf clear of the beach, so it could turn and splash its way out to deeper water.

It's Tool Time

About 2 million years ago, our ancestors learned how to make sharp cutting tools out of rocks. It's not an easy thing to do (see illustration below). With a snapping motion of the wrist, you strike a rock — called the hammer stone — against the narrow edge of the core rock you want to break, without letting go of the hammer stone. Sharp pieces of stone fly off the core rock, and these pieces can be used to cut.

Researchers asked themselves if animals could learn to make human tools. They decided to find out, and started working with Kanzi, a bonobo or pygmy chimpanzee who had already proved in language experiments that he was very smart. The first step was to give Kanzi a reason to want to make and use tools. He was given a box with a see-through lid. He could see one of his favorite treats inside the box, but a string was tied around the box to hold it shut. Kanzi watched as a human broke pieces from a core rock with a hammer rock, and then as the human used the sharp pieces to cut the string from the box. Next, Kanzi was given sharp pieces of stone so that he could cut through the string himself. Finally, it was up to Kanzi to figure out how to do the whole thing. After eight weeks, he could make small flakes from stone. But the box was tied with thick string and Kanzi needed to make bigger pieces to use to cut. The experiment seemed to have stalled.

Some Japanese herons use bait to catch fish just like human anglers. They stalk along the edges of a lake picking up insects, feathers or small pieces of bread dropped by visitors. With a flick of the head, they cast their bait onto the water then wait for the fish to rise so they can spear them with their long, sharp beaks.

One day, after looking at the core rock and then at the hard floor, Kanzi threw the rock on the floor. Stone pieces flew everywhere as the rock shattered. He grabbed a big, sharp flake and cut through the thick string. Kanzi didn't learn to make tools as the researchers expected, but he'd found his own way to solve the problem.

Teaching an animal to make and use tools is just building on what scientists observe in the wild — that some animals might be using tools to find food. Crows in the New Caledonia rainforest have been seen stripping bark from twigs and cutting them down into hooks. The crows use the hooks to scoop bugs out of trees. You might not want them in your toolbox, but they work for the crows!

Chimpanzees are very closely related to humans. So maybe it shouldn't be a very big surprise that chimps use their own tools in the wild. Even at a very young age, this chimp is experienced at using a twig the way we might use a spoon — he is poking it into a termite nest and pulling out a tasty termite snack.

It's easy to know what people think because they can tell you. Until animals can tell us what and how they think, we'll never know for sure what's going on inside their heads. It might look like dogs understand what we say, but so far, scientists have learned to communicate with animals only through sign language — either hand gestures or symbols. We haven't learned their language: they've had to learn ours!

WHO'S TALKING?

Talking to the Animals

Beside a sunlit pool in Hawaii, a researcher asks a dolphin if its Frisbee is in the water. And the dolphin answers, "Yes." How can two members of different species speak to each other? The researcher is using hand signals based on the American Sign Language that is used by deaf people, and the dolphin pushes a "Yes" paddle with its nose. The researcher is trying to find out how smart dolphins are by seeing how well they adjust to a new situation — learning a language. So far, the researcher has found that dolphins understand single words (see illustration below). Amazingly, they also understand how word order affects meaning, one of the rules you use to put sentences together. For example, dolphins know the difference between "Get the Frisbee and take it to the surfboard" and "Get the surfboard and take it to the Frisbee."

A sentence such as "Bottom pipe place-in surface hoop" might sound strange to you, but it shows that dolphins are really thinking. They recognize the difference between the pipe and the hoop, and they understand which one is on the bottom of the tank and which one on top of the water. The dolphin also has to understand that the trainer wants it to place the pipe in the hoop and not the other way around.

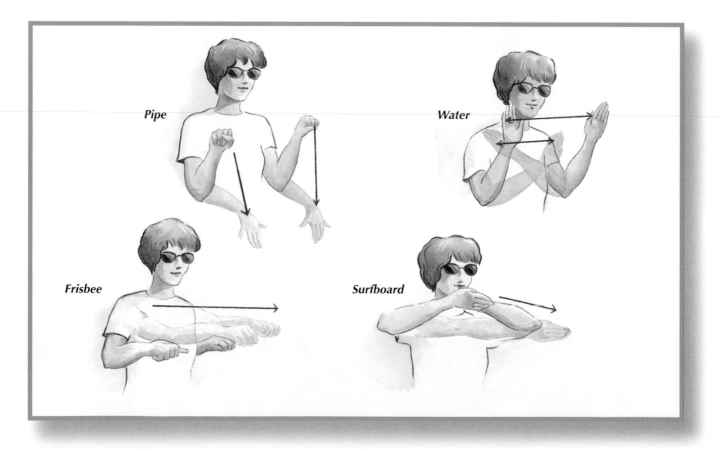

Pipe   Water

Frisbee   Surfboard

One day the researcher asked the dolphin to place the Frisbee on top of the surfboard, and the dolphin pressed the "No" paddle. The dolphin wasn't being bratty; it was just letting the researcher know that it couldn't do what he wanted. The surfboard wasn't in the pool, and the dolphin understood that it was missing. What that means is that the dolphin was using a symbol from a foreign language to call up a picture in its head of something it couldn't see. Now that's smart. In fact, the researcher thinks that dolphins might be as smart as chimpanzees.

But can dolphins communicate with humans beyond a simple "yes" or "no"? It looks like they can. In one experiment in Florida, dolphins are learning to communicate "sentences" through a keyboard installed at the bottom of their pool. It's simple stuff, but it's a beginning.

A dolphin researcher gives the "Pay attention" hand sign to two dolphin students. He has trained the dolphins to understand simple sentences. Like all dolphin trainers, he wears dark glasses so that his eyes don't give away clues about what he expects the dolphins to do or where he wants them to go.

Listen and Learn

Scientists have been teaching chimpanzees and gorillas to communicate with sign language or symbols since the 1960s. The usual method used is to teach one symbol at a time, moving on to the next symbol after one has been mastered. Scientists argued about the results. Some were convinced that the apes understood what they were communicating, but others thought that they were imitating their trainers without really understanding. Then in the 1980s Kanzi, the stone-cutting bonobo you met on page 32, put an end to many scientists' doubts.

In a lot of animal experiments, researchers discover things that they're not expecting, especially if they find that they're looking at the wrong animal. Matata, Kanzi's adoptive mother, was chosen to learn how to use a keyboard to communicate with humans. Wherever Matata went, Kanzi went too, but the researchers ignored him and didn't try to teach him anything. A year into the project, the scientists started getting hints that Kanzi was listening in on human conversations. For instance, if people talked about lights, Kanzi would run to the light switch and flip it on and off. As soon as they started watching Kanzi, it became clear that he understood human speech. Eventually, he seemed to understand so much of what was said that the researchers had to spell out some words to keep him in the dark, just as parents often do when they don't want young children to understand what they're saying.

When Kanzi flipped the switch, a light went on in the mind of the scientist in charge of the language program. It turned out that Kanzi understood 150 words of spoken English. And he'd learned them the same way a young child learns language — by listening to people talk every day and watching what they do. Instead of trying to teach Kanzi one symbol at a time, the scientist decided she should let Kanzi go on learning in his own way to see how well he did. By the time Kanzi was 10, he had the language abilities of a two-year-old child and could understand about 650 sentences. Kanzi is now in his teens, and the scientist continues to expect even more incredible things from him.

Until Kanzi was five years old, he used symbols that looked like what they stood for — the symbol for *ball* was a picture of a ball. Now Kanzi can also use symbols for things that can't be so simply pictured, such as *bad* or *good*. Can Kanzi learn to speak? No, because his throat isn't built to make all the sounds a human can. "Peanut butter" would come out as "Ee-yuh uh-er." One scientist thinks that, if chimps had throats like yours, they could learn to speak as well as a three-year-old child.

HOW DO ANIMALS TALK TO EACH OTHER?

In the animal world, there are as many ways of communicating as there are senses. Fireflies use codes of flashing lights. Some insects send vibrations through the surface of water. Humpback whales sing complex songs, which change from year to year.

Ants communicate through chemical signals and sound, and even through touch. Scout ants find food and then return to the colony and tap on the legs and antennae of forager ants to tell them how to find the food. In an experiment, scouts memorized and communicated up to eight separate pieces of information to find food in a maze — something like, "Go right, take three left turns, then right, then two left turns, then right again. There's the food!"

You walk to get places, but your dog takes a walk to catch up on all the latest doggie news. Male dogs in the neighborhood urinate on lamp posts, fire hydrants and trees to mark them as boundaries to their territories. So when a male dog stops every few seconds to sniff and pee, it's discovering who was there before him and is leaving a chemical message that says, "If you're male, go away! If you're female, come back again!"

Honeybees have one of the most complex languages on Earth, one that includes sound, movement, touch and taste, as well as an understanding of mathematics and astronomy. They use it all to give information about where food is, how far away it is, and how good it is. Scientists confirmed this by making a robot bee (left) they could operate from above. When they introduced it into a hive, it acted just like a bee with information about a food source. It made a sound to attract attention by vibrating its metal wing (at the back of the robot). Moved by the metal rod at its center, the robot gave information about the distance and location of the food by performing a dance at the correct angle to the sun. It even handed out samples of food through the syringe at far left. It must have been saying all the right things, because bees left the hive and flew straight to the food source.

This elephant's trunk fish has an amazingly large brain, and a nose to match. And these fish are wired for communication. They find their way around the murky rivers of Africa by sending out electrical signals. Different species send out different signals. They pause every few seconds to receive signals from other fish. So what do you think an elephant's trunk fish would want to keep track of — who's found food, who's taking a nap, who's having an argument and who's new in town?

Barks 'n' Purrs

One scientist claims that, on average, a dog can understand 2000 human words. You know that your dog can understand you, but how well do you understand its language? For instance, why does it bark? Barking is a warning call to the dog's pack — made up of dogs or humans — that it needs help. Usually the more noise a dog makes the less likely it is to bite, because noise is a sign of fear. A dog making growl-bark noises is telling you "I would like to attack (growl) but I need help from my pack (bark)." But a snarling dog should be treated with respect. It's telling you that it's a little afraid, but not too afraid to attack. And a completely fearless dog makes no noise at all.

Let's play!

I'm afraid and insecure.

I'm like a puppy; I won't hurt you.

Beware! I'm angry.

Hi! Good to see you!

I feel safe and I trust you.

I am content.

Watch out! I mean business.

And then there's catty talk. Everyone knows that cats say "meow" or something like that. But did you know that while cats hiss, growl and purr at each other, they only meow at humans? The high-pitched, short "me" is a happy sound of greeting, while the low-pitched "ow" is — like a dog's growl — a sound of fear or aggression. What the cat is really saying to you is, "Hello! Happy to see you. Just don't forget I've got rights around here too." Try making some short, high-pitched chirping sounds at your cat, then some low growling noises to see what effect they have on it. Now, think about your cat's name from its point of view. Is it a high-pitched, happy, chirpy name or a low-pitched growl of a name? If your cat ignores you when you call its name, perhaps it's time to change it from Bozo to Meggie.

The same scientist that would give dogs an A in language class claims that cats can only understand about 50 human words. But before you give up on communicating with your cat, remember that it's a solitary animal. Communication is a lot more important for dogs because they live in packs. So does that make dogs smarter than cats? That's something that dog-lovers and cat-lovers will be arguing about for a long time.

Talk the Talk

What is speech? It's using words to stand for objects and actions. Scientists have taught many animals to communicate with humans, but there's only one animal that can make recognizable words come out of its mouth as real speech. Meet Alex, the African gray parrot. Language experiments with Alex started when a scientist noted that some songbirds sing different songs in different situations, just as people sing "Happy Birthday" at a party and the national anthem at the start of a sports event.

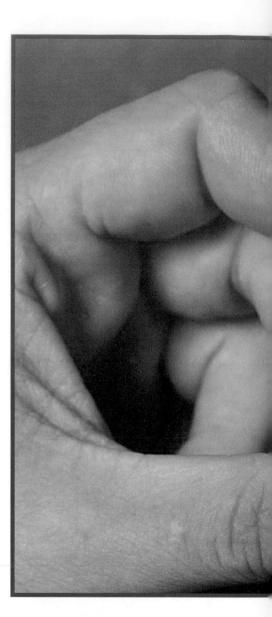

Alex knows when he's told to sit on his chair that it's time to work. Alex's competitive nature helps his trainer. When she wants to teach Alex a new word, she'll ask a human "student" what an object is called. Then she will praise the student and hand over the object at the correct answer. Alex likes to be the center of his trainer's attention, so he competes with the other student to learn the new word and get the reward.

In the lab, Alex shows he understands that certain words stand for certain objects, as well as actions and ideas. If you hold up two different-sized keys and ask, "Alex, how many?" after a pause he'll say "Two." If you ask, "Which is bigger?" he'll tell you. And if you hold up a blue block and a blue key and ask what they have in common, he'll say "Color." Or if they have nothing in common he'll tell you that, too.

What Alex says is as important as the fact that he talks. It seems to tell us he can understand difficult concepts like size, similarity and difference. Some scientists feel Alex's language training might have uncovered an ability that parrots, and other animals, use in the wild. But we'll continue to find it very hard to figure out how smart animals are until we find a way to communicate with them.

Alex can speak because his throat is designed to make many kinds of sounds, including the sounds that we make. But being able to say the right words properly doesn't necessarily equal having the brains to carry on a complicated conversation. It's taken Alex more than ten years to learn about 70 words and simple phrases such as "Come here," "Want to go" and "How many?"

Animals Who Count

All this talk about language brings us back to where we started — with numbers and symbols. A chimp named Sarah has proven that she understands the connection between numbers and the symbols we use to represent them (such as 1, 2, 3). She has even gone two better than the raven you learned about in the first chapter: she can count up to eight, and she can also do simple addition. One day Sarah was shown a plate containing one gumdrop, and one containing seven gumdrops. She was supposed to point to the plate she wanted to give to her companion Sheba.

Researchers into animal smarts often use animals they've had a lot of success with to teach other animals. So they work with their star students and younger animals at the same time. These two pictures show Sarah's gumdrop experiment duplicated with Sheba and a young male chimpanzee named Bobby.

You'd think that Sarah would choose the plate containing the fewest gumdrops, but greed got in the way. Sarah kept pointing to the plate with the most gumdrops, and became very upset when they were given to Sheba. When the gumdrops were replaced by numbers on cards, Sarah was finally able to get it right. The sight of all that candy she wanted so much must have wiped out her ability to think her way through the problem.

Sarah and Charles the gorilla (remember him from the introduction?) don't use language, but both of them can count. Their use of numbers shows that they grasp the logic of something standing for something else, and that's the basis of language. Maybe this kind of thinking has to be in an animal's head before it can learn language. And animals are showing us in all kinds of ways that there is much more in their heads than we might have believed.

Animals can do many things we used to think only humans could do. But will they be able to develop them further, as we have? It's a question that will keep scientists busy for a long time to come.

It seems as if a sea lion named Rio can do some complicated reasoning. Rio was shown three groups of photos, and was asked to match a picture from group A with one from group B. Then she was asked to match the group B picture with one from group C. Now for the tricky part. Could she pair up the picture from group A with the one from group C without seeing the B picture again? Rio aced the test. Scientists call this equivalence thinking, like the math used to show that if A = B and B = C, then A must also equal C.

Index